I Go to the Garden

Learning the Hard G Sound

Kevin Sarkisian

Phonics
for the
REAL World™

Rosen Classroom Books and Materials™
New York

I go to the garden.

My garden has a gate.

I go to the garden to plant seeds.

I go to the garden to look at a bud.

I go to the garden to look at a bug.

I go to the garden to take a nap.

I go to the garden to read a book.

I go to the garden to get flowers.

I go to the garden to play a game.

I have a good time in my garden!

Word List

game

garden

gate

get

go

good

Instructional Guide

Note to Instructors:
One of the essential skills that enable a young child to read is the ability to associate letter-sound symbols and blend these sounds to form words. Phonics instruction can teach children a system that will help them decode unfamiliar words and, in turn, enhance their word-recognition skills. We offer a phonics-based series of books that are easy to read and understand. Each book pairs words and pictures that reinforce specific phonetic sounds in a logical sequence. Topics are based on curriculum goals appropriate for early readers in the areas of science, social studies, and health.

Letter/Sound: g – Have the child listen to the following sentences and tell which words begin with the same sound: *Golf is a fine game to play. A silly goose got into the garden. Mom told the girls to stop giggling.* As the child responds, list initial consonant **g** words on the chalkboard. Have the child underline the initial **g** in each word. Continue with sentences using other initial **g** words, such as *go, get, gate, goat, game, gas, ghost, good,* etc. Prepare flash cards with the listed initial consonant **g** words. Have the child match the flash cards to the listed words. Ask them to define the words and/or use the words in sentences of their own.

Phonics Activities: Pronounce the following pairs of words: *game – guard, gum – go, fed – fish, girl – gate, fall – five, gab – get, gill – gap, fine – farm, fan – fit,* etc. Have the child hold up a card with **g** written on it if each word in the pair begins with consonant **g**. Have the child hold up a card with **f** written on it if each word in the pair begins with **f**. As the child responds, write the initial **g** and **f** words in separate columns. Have the child name and underline the initial consonant in each word.

• Provide pictures of items whose names begin with **m**, **t**, **p**, and **g**. Have the child write the correct letter beneath each picture. Follow with a similar activity, this time focusing on initial **b**, **d**, **f**, and **g**.

• List one-syllable words used in *I Go to the Garden* and in previous stories. Create additional words by changing the initial consonants in these words. (Example: The word *nap* can become *gap, tap, map,* or *cap.*)

Additional Resources:
• Florian, Douglas. *The Vegetable Garden.* San Diego, CA: Harcourt, 1994.
• Lerner, Carol. *My Backyard Garden.* New York: Morrow Avon, 1998.
• Lovejoy, Sharon. *Roots, Shoots, Buckets & Boots.* New York: Workman Publishing Company, Inc., 1999.
• Smith, Maggie. *This Is Your Garden.* New York: Crown Books for Young Readers, 1998.

Published in 2002 by The Rosen Publishing Group, Inc.
29 East 21st Street, New York, NY 10010

Book Design: Haley Wilson

Photo Credits: Cover © Gay Bumgarner/Index Stock; p. 3 © Omni Photo Communications, Inc./Index Stock; p. 5 © Carolyn Bross/FPG International; p. 7 © Chris Lowe/FPG International; p. 9 © Dave Ryan/Index Stock; p. 11 © ChromaZone Images/Index Stock; p. 13 © Caroline Woodham/International Stock; p. 15 © Telegraph Colour Library/FPG International; p. 17 © Dusty Willison/International Stock; p. 19 © Richard Wood/Index Stock; p. 21 © VCG/FPG International.

Library of Congress Cataloging-in-Publication Data

Sarkisian, Kevin.
 I go to the garden : learning the hard G sound / Kevin Sarkisian.— 1st ed.
    p. cm. — (Power phonics/phonics for the real world)
 ISBN 0-8239-5907-4 (lib. bdg.)
 ISBN 0-8239-8252-1 (pbk.)
 6-pack ISBN 0-8239-9220-9
 1. Children's gardens—Juvenile literature. [1. Gardens.
 2. Vocabulary.] I. Title. II. Series.
 SB457 .S28 2001
 635—dc21
                                              00-013193

Manufactured in the United States of America